How Great Thou Art

a word-and-picture guide into the wonderful
world God created for His glory and our enjoyment!

by

Nathanael Olson

T5-DHH-308

"This natural universe is a vast
autograph album with its pages
made up of mountains and
molecules and motes and atoms;
and God's signature is written,
sometimes very small and
sometimes hugely large, on
every page of it."

Dr. Robert G. Lee

Editorial Director, James Kuse
Managing Editor, Ralph Luedtke
Photographic Editor, Gerald Koser
Production Editor, Stuart L. Zyduck

An *ideals* Publication
Third Printing
ISBN 0-89542-059-7 395

The Story of Creation

In the beginning God created the heaven and the earth. And the earth was without form, and void; and darkness *was* upon the face of the deep. And the Spirit of God moved upon the face of the waters.

The First Day

And God said, Let there be light: and there was light. And God saw the light, that *it was* good: and God divided the light from the darkness. And God called the light Day, and the darkness he called Night. And the evening and the morning were the first day.

The Second Day

And God said, Let there be a firmament in the midst of the waters, and let it divide the waters from the waters. And God made the firmament, and divided the waters which *were* under the firmament from the waters which *were* above the firmament: and it was so. And God called the firmament Heaven. And the evening and the morning were the second day.

The Third Day

And God said, Let the waters under the heaven be gathered together unto one place, and let the dry *land* appear: and it was so. And God called the dry *land* Earth; and the gathering together of the waters called he Seas: and God saw that *it was* good. And God said, Let the earth bring forth grass, the herb yielding seed, *and* the fruit tree yielding fruit after his kind, whose seed *is* in itself, upon the earth: and it was so. And the earth brought forth grass, *and* herb yielding seed after his kind, and the tree yielding fruit, whose seed was in itself, after his kind: and God saw that *it was* good. And the evening and the morning were the third day.

The Fourth Day

And God said, Let there be lights in the firmament of the heaven to divide the day from the night; and let them be for signs, and for seasons, and for days, and years: And let them be for lights in the firmament of the heaven to give light upon the earth: and it was so. And God made two great lights; the greater light to rule the day, and the lesser light to rule the night: *he made* the stars also. And God set them in the firmament of the heaven to give light upon the earth, and to rule over the day and over the night, and to divide the light from the darkness: and God saw that *it was* good. And the evening and the morning were the fourth day.

The Fifth Day

And God said, Let the waters bring forth abundantly the moving creature that hath life, and fowl *that* may fly above the earth in the open firmament of heaven. And God created great whales, and every living creature that moveth, which the waters brought forth abundantly, after their kind, and every winged fowl after his kind: and God saw that *it was* good. And God blessed them, saying, Be fruitful, and multiply, and fill the waters in the seas, and let fowl multiply in the earth. And the evening and the morning were the fifth day.

IDEALS PUBLISHING CORP., MILWAUKEE, WIS. 53201
© COPYRIGHT MCMLXXIV, PRINTED AND BOUND IN U.S.A.

The Sixth Day

And God said, Let the earth bring forth the living creature after his kind, cattle, and creeping thing, and beast of the earth after his kind: and it was so. And God made the beast of the earth after his kind, and cattle after their kind, and every thing that creepeth upon the earth after his kind: and God saw that *it was* good. And God said, Let us make man in our image, after our likeness: and let them have dominion over the fish of the sea, and over the fowl of the air, and over the cattle, and over all the earth, and over every creeping thing that creepeth upon the earth. So God created man in his *own* image, in the image of God created he him; male and female created he them. And God blessed them, and God said unto them, Be fruitful, and multiply, and replenish the earth, and subdue it: and have dominion over the fish of the sea, and over the fowl of the air, and over every living thing that moveth upon the earth. And God said, Behold, I have given you every herb bearing seed, which is upon the face of all the earth, and every tree, in the which *is* the fruit of a tree yielding seed; to you it shall be for meat. And to every beast of the earth, and to every fowl of the air, and to every thing that creepeth upon the earth, wherein *there is* life, *I have given* every green herb for meat: and it was so. And God saw every thing that he had made, and, behold, *it was* very good. And the evening and the morning were the sixth day.

The Seventh Day

Thus the heavens and the earth were finished, and all the host of them. And on the seventh day God ended his work which he had made; and he rested on the seventh day from all his work which he had made.

Genesis 1:1 through 2:2

Stars

"He telleth the number of the stars;
he calleth them all by their names."

Psalm 147:4

With these words, the Psalmist underscores God's concern for His creation. Divinely inspired, he tells of God's infinite knowledge — "He telleth the *number* of the stars." Then he quickly adds a sentence showing God's personal concern — "He calleth them all by their *names*." Greatness and goodness combine in the nature of God!

Thousands of years ago, God asked Abraham, "Look now toward heaven, and tell the stars, if thou be able to number them:" (Genesis 15:5). Of course, Abraham couldn't. Neither can modern man. It is believed now that perhaps 6,000 stars can be seen without a telescope and countless more with one. Yet no one knows for sure how many stars are really out there. (Astronomers estimate there are 100 to 200 billion stars in just the galaxy where our sun is situated!)

Although most stars appear white to the naked eye, certain of the brightest of the variable ones are red as a drop of blood, others show red and orange tints, or blue and green. The color is considered to be in direct function of the surface temperature of these stars.

Speaking of color, the bright orange star we see in the western sky at sunset is Arcturus. During the Chicago World's Fair of 1933, a telescope at Yerkes Observatory was used to focus this star's beams on an electric eye. The electric eye, in turn, switched on the lights of the mammoth fairgrounds. Those in charge were proving a memorable point. Because Arcturus is 40 light-years away from the earth, its beams, received in 1933, had originated 40 years before when Arcturus shone down on the first Chicago World's Fair in 1893!

Each generation seems to be star-struck. The ancient prophet, Daniel, gives this word of advice to any would-be star. "They that be wise shall shine as the brightness of the firmament; and they that turn many to righteousness, as the stars for ever and ever." (Daniel 12:3)

One starry night, Abraham Lincoln said to his friend, Captain Gilbert J. Greene: "I never behold them (the stars) that I do not feel that I am looking into the face of God. I can see how it might be possible for a man to look down upon the earth and be an atheist but I cannot conceive how he could look up into the heavens and say there is no God."

Light and Color

Light is so vital to life that the first act of God in creation was to say, "Let there be light." (Genesis 1:3)

Without light, the chlorophyll of the leaf would not function. Without plants, animals and man would starve. Our very existence is dependent upon "The Father of lights, with whom is no variableness, neither shadow of turning." (James 1:17)

Without light, we could not enjoy the beauty of earth and sky for we see only the light which bounces off these objects. When light is absent we see nothing!

Jesus, well aware of the natural world He and the Father created, told the people of His day, "I am the light of the world: he that followeth me shall not walk in darkness, but shall have the light of life." (John 8:12)

On another occasion, He told his followers, "You are the light of the world." In Matthew 5:16, He commanded, "Let your light so shine before men, that they may see your good works, and glorify your Father which is in heaven."

One of Christ's later followers, Sir Isaac Newton, began a series of experiments to investigate the nature of color which is intimately associated with light. God inspired the 23-year-old scientist to place a prism in a beam of sunlight shining into a dark room through a small hole in a shutter. Newton was delighted to discover that the beam of light produced the colors of the solar spectrum — red, orange, yellow, green, blue, indigo and violet. Later, using a second prism, the young scientist recombined these colors and found that they produced a white light. He then knew that light — white to the eye — was, in reality, a miraculous combination of all the spectrum colors!

What a bright, colorful world God made when He said, "Let there be light!"

Lightning

"Don't stand under a tree during a storm!" Most of us have had parents who gave us this warning. And it is good advice, especially if the tree in question is an oak. This tree holds a large amount of water, which, when heated by the lightning, turns into steam and explodes. This doesn't take long because the power of lightning is 500 million kilowatts!

What causes lightning? Simply put, it is an exchange between negative and positive electrical charges. The great turbulence in the storm cloud generates negative charges in the middle regions while positive charges remain on top of the cloud. As the storm cloud drifts above planet earth, the positive charges on earth build up and climb trees, towers, and other high spots trying to reach the negative charges in the cloud. (Remember the old law that unlike charges attract?)

Actually then, lightning does not shoot *down* from the clouds. Rather, it hurtles *up* — from earth to heaven. On some occasions, lightning jumps from cloud to cloud.

Lightning, however, serves more than a dramatic purpose. Benjamin Franklin, in 1752, with Leyden Jar, with string and kite in hand, proved that lightning is electricity.

Lightning is also what provokes the chemical reaction necessary to turn the insoluble nitrogen of the air into soluble nitrogen for the earth — vital to the growth of plants.

The Psalmist gave another reason for lightning's existence — to help in the distribution of water. Psalm 135:7 says, "He causeth the vapors to ascend from the ends of the earth; he maketh lightnings for the rain; he bringeth the wind out of his treasuries." Water, weighing 800 times that of the air, has to be raised miles above the earth and held there against the law of gravity. How does God do it?

First, "He causeth vapors to ascend." Sunlight changes heavy rain into molecules of vapor that rise and float lightly in clouds.

Second, "He maketh lightning for the rain." These electrical discharges unite the molecules of vapor into raindrops, heavy enough to be gravitated to earth.

Third, "He bringeth the wind out of his treasuries." God uses the wind to keep the vapor moving all over the earth so that all the rain would not just fall back into the sea or lake from where the vapor originally came. God is the master of recycling.

Great *is* the Lord, and greatly to be praised; and his greatness *is* unsearchable." (Psalm 145:3)

"For as the lightning cometh out of the east, and shineth even unto the west; so shall also the coming of the Son of man be."

Matthew 24:27

The Sun

The Moon

God, the Author of light, desires his people to not live in darkness, either physically or spiritually.

On the fourth day of creation, God put the sun in the heavens. Genesis 1:16 describes it as "the greater light to rule the day." Science tells us that the sun is the largest and the brightest of the stars visible to the naked eye, although it ranks among the smallest and the faintest of the stars. The reason it appears so big and bright to earth dwellers is because of its nearness to our planet, only 93 million miles away. The next nearest star is almost 300,000 times as far removed!

Inspired by the light from the sun and the light of God's love, John Keble wrote:

"Sun of my soul! Thou Savior dear,
It is not night if Thou be near;
Oh, may no earthborn cloud arise
To hide Thee from Thy servant's eyes!"

God never leaves anything half done. On the same day He created the sun to rule the day, He fashioned the moon, "the lesser light to rule the night." (Genesis 1:16).

Science verifies that the moon is definitely the lesser of the two. In fact, the sun is about 465,000 times as bright as the moon.

Yet, in spite of its lack of brilliance, the moon has fascinated man throughout history. It has been worshiped and credited with many claims that science says are false. Only one major belief about the moon has born the test of time and science — the movement of the earth's tides *is* directly affected by the moon.

Today we know more about the moon than ever before because, in 1969, two American astronauts climbed down the ladder of their lunar module and bounced across the surface of the moon! There they found less than one inch of meteoritic dust, moon rocks, and other amazing things out of this world!

How great is the Creator of the sun, the moon, and the stars!

Weather

A resident of Hawaii told a person from the Midwest, "The weather varies very little in the islands."

"How terrible!" the Midwesterner exclaimed. "I wouldn't know how to begin a conversation if I couldn't talk about the weather." Talking about the weather is big business. The United States Weather Bureau in Washington, D.C. receives daily observations made at more than 12,000 locations in the U.S.A. and adjacent waters.

The highest temperature recorded in the U.S.A. was 134 degrees at Death Valley, California in 1913. Forty-one years later, in 1954, Rogers Pass, Montana recorded the lowest temperature — a biting 70 degrees below zero!

The Bible tells us, "He bringeth the wind out of his treasuries" (Psalm 135:7) and Matthew 5:45 adds another fact. "He sendeth rain on the just and on the unjust." Moisture and the speed and the direction of the wind greatly affect the weather. Therefore, we must conclude that God is the Giver of weather, and that our complaining about it is, in reality, finding fault with His plans. How much better it is to greet each day with the enthusiasm of the Psalmist: "This *is* the day which the Lord hath made; we will rejoice and be glad in it." (Psalm 118:24)

In this existence, dry or wet
Will overtake the best of men;
Some little skift of clouds'll shet
The sun off now and then.

They hain't no sense, as I can see
In mortals such as us, to be
A-faultin' Natchur's wise intents,
And lockin' horns with Providence.

It hain't no use to grumble and complane,
It's jest as cheap and easy to rejoice;
When God sorts out the weather and sends rain,
W'y, rain's my choice!

James Whitcomb Riley

13

Air

Because of air pollution, we have become increasingly aware of how vital is the thin layer of air which surrounds planet earth. Obviously, human life could not exist if God did not graciously provide air — composed of oxygen (21%), nitrogen (78%), and minute mixtures of other gases.

If oxygen were the only element present, our earth would go up in flames. (Oxygen is the gas that causes substances to burn.)

If nitrogen were the only element in the air, nothing would burn. It extinguishes a flame quickly.

If only nitrogen and oxygen were present, no plants could adequately grow. Plants must have carbon dioxide. Yet this is the very gas that means death to all other life, including man. God, however, mixed carbon dioxide in such minute amounts that it would not harm man while permitting plants to get adequate amounts for growth. Who but an all-wise Creator could mix oxygen, nitrogen, carbon dioxide, argon and other gases making earth a safe place for man, animals, and plants?

The Apostle Paul taught: "God giveth to all life, and breath, and all things. In him we live, and move, and have our being." (Acts 17:25 and 28)

Our very breath is dependent on the mercy and provision of our Heavenly Father!

Sunrise . . . Sunset

The greatness and goodness of God is gloriously evident in each day's sunrise and sunset.

The sunrise is a flaming reminder that "today is the first day of the rest of your life."

The sunset is a radiant ending to any day, no matter how drab or delightful it may have been!

The secret of a successful life then, is learning to live it in "day-tight compartments." The Bible promises, "As thy days *so shall* thy strength be." (Deuteronomy 33:25)

Jesus said, "When it is evening, ye say, *It will be* fair weather: for the sky is red. And in the morning, *It will be* foul weather to-day: for the sky is red and lowering. Ye can discern the face of the sky; but can ye not *discern* the signs of the times?" (Matthew 16:2 and 3)

"The sun also ariseth, and the sun goeth down, and hasteth to his place where he arose."

Ecclesiastes 1:5

The Eagle

Standing three feet in height, with a wingspread of seven feet, the bald eagle looks its part as "the king of birds." Because its general color is dark, its white head just looks bald.

The eagle mates for life. Its nest, an "eyrie," is built near the top of the highest tree available. No temporary shelter, it is lived in year in and year out. The only "home improvement" each year is a new top of sticks.

The eagle, however, is more at home in the air than in the nest. It soars gracefully, majestically, and drifts, wings almost motionless, in the air thermals.

When its offspring are three months old, they are toppled out of the nest and fall earthward — screaming violently, feeling that destruction is imminent. Then the parent bird sweeps under them and catches them on her giant wings, giving them breathing time before their next lesson in eagle flying!

Moses used this fact to illustrate the way God dealt with his people back then. "As an eagle stirreth up her nest, fluttereth over her young, spreadeth abroad her wings, taketh them, beareth them on her wings: So the Lord alone did lead him." (Deuteronomy 32:11 and 12)

The eagle, America's emblem, has inspired generations of its citizens. Back around the Civil War days, Chief Blue Sky captured an eagle and gave him to a white man in exchange for five bushels of corn. Named "Old Abe" (after President Lincoln), this eagle was bought for $2.50 by the 8th Wisconsin Volunteers. They took him along as their mascot. He went through four years of war, took part in 22 battles, but was never seriously injured. Finally "Old Abe" was given to the state of Wisconsin and died of old age in 1881.

Thousands of years ago the Prophet Isaiah wrote, "They that wait upon the Lord shall renew *their* strength; they shall mount up with wings as eagles." (Isaiah 40:31) What a wonderful promise in these days of stress and strain!

Birds

Examine the bodies of birds; consider that strange something you cannot see — instinct — and you will readily understand that God designed birds for flight. Robins, meadowlarks, and nearly 8,600 other distinct species now in existence are destined for the skies!

Jesus liked to refer to feathered friends in his teachings. Underscoring God's concern for people, the Lord asked, "Are not five sparrows sold for two farthings, and not one of them is forgotten before God? Fear not therefore: ye are of more value than many sparrows." (Luke 12:6 and 7) An old poem by Elizabeth Cheney relates the following imaginative conversation:

> Said the sparrow to the robin:
> "I should really like to know
> Why these anxious human beings
> Rush about and worry so."
>
> Said the robin to the sparrow:
> "Friend, I think that it must be
> That they have no Heavenly Father
> Such as cares for you and me!"

"Behold the fowls of the air: for they sow not, neither do they reap, nor gather into barns; yet your heavenly Father feedeth them. Are ye not much better than they?"

Matthew 6:26

The Turkey

The turkey might have been famous for more than its Thanksgiving Day edibility if the Continental Congress of June 20, 1782 had followed Benjamin Franklin's suggestion to make it America's national bird. Its beautiful body plumage and the red, white and blue of its head, coupled with the fact that it is generally considered a native of America, should have swung the votes in its favor. Instead the eagle won.

The turkey, however, is far from forgotten. Approximately 900 million are raised annually. A turkey dinner has become synonymous with Thanksgiving Day.

There is a historical reason for this association. The grateful Pilgrims in Plymouth found their hearts pulsating with sincere gratitude for the plenteous harvest of 1621. (During the previous winter, half of the colony had died.)

Overjoyed at the change in circumstances, Governor Bradford invited the Indian Chief Massasoit to take part in their festival of thanksgiving. The chief came, accompanied by a 90-man regiment of soldiers!

When the ten women cooks were told, "Guess who's coming to dinner?" they complained that they didn't have enough food for so many unexpected guests. The Indian men, however, saved the day. They gave the cooks five deer and several turkeys! These naturally were wild turkeys.

The domestic turkey came to America from Europe. No one knows for certain how its name was coined, although it seems possible that the turkey could have been confused with the guinea cock which had been brought out of Africa into Europe through Turkey. Perhaps this is how Tom received his last name!

May Tom Turkey ever remind us, as individuals and as a nation, to express our gratitude to God, the Giver of all gifts. "In every thing give thanks," wrote the Apostle Paul, "for this is the will of God in Christ Jesus concerning you."
(I Thessalonians 5:18)

Psalm 23

The Lord *is* my shepherd; I shall not want.

He maketh me to lie down in green pastures:
he leadeth me beside the still waters.

He restoreth my soul: he leadeth me in the
paths of righteousness for his name's sake.

Yea, though I walk through the valley of the
shadow of death, I will fear no evil: for thou
art with me; thy rod and thy staff they
comfort me.

Thou preparest a table before me in the
presence of mine enemies: thou anointest
my head with oil; my cup runneth over.

Surely goodness and mercy shall follow me
all the days of my life: and I will dwell in
the house of the Lord for ever.

Sheep

God, who sees and understands human nature, compares people not to sly foxes or busy beavers but to wayward sheep! No other animal is as helpless when left on its own. A sheep needs the constant tender care of the shepherd. Jesus has promised, "I am the good Shepherd." (John 10:14)

No other animal becomes so hopelessly lost. A dog or a cat can find its way home, even though it may involve traveling hundreds of miles. But a sheep has no sense of direction; when it is lost, it's lost until the shepherd finds it. "All we like sheep have gone astray." (Isaiah 53:6)

David, called from tending flocks of sheep to be King of Israel, drew from his experiences as a shepherd to write the beloved Twenty-third Psalm. Note such phrases as:

"Beside the still waters." A sheep is a very poor swimmer so naturally fears a fast-flowing stream.

"Thou anointest my head with oil." The shepherd uses oil, with its healing properties, to help ease the hurts and bruises a sheep encounters during the course of a day.

As we face the problems of everyday living, may we take comfort in knowing that the shepherd goes *before* his sheep. Then we can sing: "He leadeth me, O blessed thought!"

The Dog

Two qualities the Bible urges man to manifest — friendliness and faithfulness — seem to be inborn traits of most of the canines. Perhaps this accounts for the dog's perennial popularity. There are 29 to 35 million dogs in the United States alone, and an estimated 120 to 150 million around the world.

They come in all shapes, sizes and colors. The Irish wolfhound stands 37 inches tall; the toy poodle is only eight inches high. The St. Bernard often exceeds 200 pounds; the chihuahua registers a mere one and a half pounds. They all belong to dog-kind, but their physical and tempermental differences are very apparent.

Dogs cannot see colors, just shades of grey. Their hearing is excellent. Their sense of smell is the keenest of their senses.

Probably the first animal domesticated by man, the dog has earned the reputation of being "man's best friend." Who can forget the love of Lassie, the golden collie, or the fierce loyalty of Rin-Tin-Tin, the German shepherd?

Or Chips, the mixed husky and collie who served with General Patton's Seventh Army in the Sicily landing? One day, the dog and his master were pinned down by an Italian machine gun. The soldier could not move, but somehow Chips tore away, jumped the crew in savage rage, frightening them into surrender. Later, Chips was recommended for the Distinguished Service Cross for bravery.

In Paris, France, stands a large monument marking the grave of Barry, a famous St. Bernard. The inscription states that in 12 years of faithful service, Barry saved 41 lives!

Friendliness and faithfulness, the two traits so desperately needed today, are generously shown by the nearly 400 varieties of dogs which God has given for our enjoyment and companionship.

The Horse

God invested many qualities in one animal when he fashioned the horse.

Beauty — head high, hide shining, mane flowing in the wind!

Strength — long, muscular legs, strong to pull or run. Or for defense. Who can withstand the kick of a horse?

Efficiency — sharp ears, keen eyes, wide nostrils to breathe easily, quick, obedient — once the favorite and the fastest way of travel for hunters, soldiers, and pioneers.

Although the automobile has taken the place of the horse for most land travel, the influence of the horse still lingers on. Phrases such as "horseless carriage" and "iron horse" add color to conversation. Western movies and telecasts are still popular. Books about horses are still read. Will the automobile ever inspire a story to match *Black Beauty*?

America currently has around eight million horses. In 1971, the Congress of the United States passed a law to protect the wild horse. Today, less than 20,000 roam the American West.

The Bible speaks often of the horse, usually in the sense of a war-horse. The Book of Revelation describes mankind's final battle, Armageddon, as a conflict fought on horseback. When that day comes, the world will once more be aware of how vital the horse is to the history of man.

Deer

The unique designs of God are clearly seen in the way he fashioned the graceful deer.

Born in the month of May or June, the fawn quickly adapts to its environment. When its mother goes off to feed, the baby deer is ready to cope with life's problems, although it is only a few days old. It instinctively knows how to freeze — laying motionless without so much as the twitch of an ear. Marked with white spots, the fawn is well camouflaged as light and shade interchange with the swaying of tree branches. It gives no odor.

The busy doe, the mother, tears off food in a hurry, filling her paunch with leaves and bark, digesting them later in her four-chambered stomach when she has the time to enjoy some peace and safety.

While all this is going on, the stately buck, the father, is proudly growing his set of antlers — not hollow creations such as horns are, but solid bone. Under a velvet protection, the buck's bloodstream continually feeds this giant headgear which grows amazingly fast from April through October. November is the rutting season when the buck will need strong antlers for defense. Another buck may challenge him for one of his does! He may win or his antlers may interlock with his rival in such a way that both bucks may die of exhaustion and starvation.

If the buck survives the rutting season, his antlers will automatically drop off by the end of December. They have fulfilled their purpose.

Perhaps the Psalmist had God's care of the deer in mind when he wrote, "Thou *art* my hiding place; thou shalt preserve me from trouble." (Psalm 32:7) In verse one of Psalm 42, we *know* the writer had a deer in mind when he exclaimed, "As the hart panteth after the water brooks, so panteth my soul after thee, O God."

"Thou art
my hiding
place;
thou shalt
preserve
me from
trouble."

What is the largest living land animal?
What animal has the keenest sense of smell?
What animal eats 300 to 600 pounds of food every day?
What animal is essential to a zoo or a circus?
You guessed it! The elephant.

Elephant

He *is* the largest animal on land, probably weighing in at 200 pounds at birth and growing to a possible weight of six tons and a height of 12 feet. A vegetarian, he spends most of the day looking for hundreds of pounds of food.

Because of his keen sense of smell, the elephant has been a popular companion of man when hunting in the areas where tigers roam. When the elephant sniffs the tigers, the hunters, riding on the elephant's back in a "howdah" (a saddle), would take aim and kill the unsuspecting tiger.

The elephant, however, is most famous for his trunk — a versatile tool containing no bone. Its more than 40,000 muscles make the trunk flexible at every point. It is used for eating and drinking. It is the elephant's built-in shower. He uses it to spray water all over his back. And with it, he pushes heavy objects or defends himself. He can throw an attacking tiger to the ground and then trample it to death. He also wards off enemies with his tusks which may weigh over 200 pounds and measure more than 11 feet in length.

When domesticated, the elephant becomes one of the most gentle and patient of God's creation. People can ride on his head or his back; children can be carried by his trunk.

Although the Bible does not specifically name the elephant, it does refer to ivory — "the ivory house" (I Kings 22:39) and the rich who "lie upon beds of ivory." (Amos 6:4)

When looking at this giant animal, we are motivated to exclaim with the Psalmist, "Great *is* our Lord, and of great power!" (Psalm 147:5) "All thy works shall praise thee, O Lord." (Psalm 145:10)

The Ocean

O the lure of the ocean! It calls children to make sand castles and listen to seashells . . . it urges young lovers to run barefoot along its beaches, the salt breeze in their glowing faces . . . it persuades hurried, worried adults to come, relax, to the rhythm of the waves . . . it comforts the aged with happy memories of family togetherness, when the children, now grown and gone, delighted in picnics by the sea.

The lure of the ocean is as endless as its waves!

Yet there is a restlessness to its continual ebb and flow. The Prophet Isaiah wrote, ". . . The wicked are like the troubled sea, when it cannot rest . . . There is no peace, saith my God, to the wicked." (Isaiah 57:20,21)

The story, however, does not end there. The New Testament portrays Jesus Christ, the Prince of Peace, as Lord and Master over any contrary

circumstance, any rebellious heart. To the troubled waters of Galilee, He said, "Peace, be still" and there was a great calm.

Today, His words, when loved and obeyed, bring peace to a soul as quickly as they brought a calm to the troubled sea of yesteryear.

"They that go down to the sea in ships, that do business in great waters; These see the works of the Lord, and his wonders in the deep. For He commandeth, and raiseth the stormy wind, which lifteth up the waves thereof. They mount up to the heaven, they go down again to the depths: their soul is melted because of trouble. They reel to and fro, and stagger like a drunken man, and are at their wit's end. Then they cry unto the Lord in their trouble, and he bringeth them out of their distresses. He maketh the storm a calm, so that the waves thereof are still." (Psalm 107:23-29)

The Four Seasons

"While the earth remaineth, seedtime and harvest, and cold and heat, and summer and winter, and day and night shall not cease." (Genesis 8:22) Such was God's promise to Noah after the catastrophic flood.

WINTER — when nature sleeps

"Earth is at rest and quiet."

Zechariah 1:11

"I am the resurrection, and the life."

John 11:25

SPRING — when nature awakens

SUMMER — when nature works

"Establish thou the work
of our hands."

Psalm 90:17

"To every thing there is a
season, and a time to every
purpose under the heaven.
He hath made every thing
beautiful in his time."

Ecclesiastes 3:1 and 11

AUTUMN — when nature relaxes

Wheat

"Give us this day our daily bread" the Lord Jesus taught His followers to pray. Bread, made from wheat, is a necessity of life, and it comes from God's loving hand. The storekeeper gets the bread from the baker, the baker gets the flour from the miller, the miller gets the wheat from the farmer, and the farmer gets the wheat from God.

Almost half of the 3,554,000,000 acres of cultivated land in this world is used to grow cereals. About 536,800,000 acres — one-third of the cultivated land — grows wheat. When whole wheat is used in baking, it provides the consumer with five important items: carbohydrates, protein, fats, minerals and some vitamins.

The wheat kernel itself, composed of water, carbohydrates, protein, fat, minerals and crude fibers, is a very productive creation. In an experiment in England, *one* kernel of wheat was planted in an ideal environment. As soon as it produced a harvest, the additional kernels were planted and their harvest, in turn, was planted. Continued over a period of two years, the original kernel eventually brought forth 32,500 grains of wheat!

The Lord Jesus knew how prolific wheat is when he taught: "Except a corn of wheat fall into the ground and die, it abideth alone: but if it die, it bringeth forth much fruit." (John 12:24) Because of His sacrifice, we see the golden harvest of millions of believers in Christ — here at home and in faraway places with strange-sounding names.

Many years ago Henry Ward Beecher, the great clergyman, told of a discovery that some archaeologists had made. They had found and opened an ancient Egyptian tomb. Inside were kernels of wheat which had lain there for 3,000 years, doing nothing but keeping company with dead mummies. The discoverers planted these kernels and soon they produced a harvest! With silver-tongued oratory about man's immortality, Dr. Beecher concluded, "If wheat will keep as long as that, I am sure man will. When God breaks the seal . . . the germ will grow again!"

"Prairie Cathedrals"*

Towering high above the rolling plains,
Reaching toward a sweep of azure sky,
Prairie Cathedrals stand with massive frames,
First to be seen by the wanderer's eye.
No well-learned bishops within their rugged walls
But rather men, strong backed, with calloused hands,
No well-dressed visitors within their halls,
Just men in overalls, fresh from the land.

The pews are bins, the members golden grain,
The choir lofts are dusty rafters high;
The choir members, lifting the refrain,
Are sparrows from the open sky.
The wind's the organ, changing keys,
The reeds are splinters clinging to the boards;
Time spent within cathedrals such as these
Provides a service no other church afford!

Nathanael Olson
Copyright 1974
Nat Olson Publications

In Europe, the first building to be seen in any town is the cathedral. On the Canadian prairies, where the author was reared, the grain elevator is the first building to greet the eye. Hence the title, "Prairie Cathedrals."

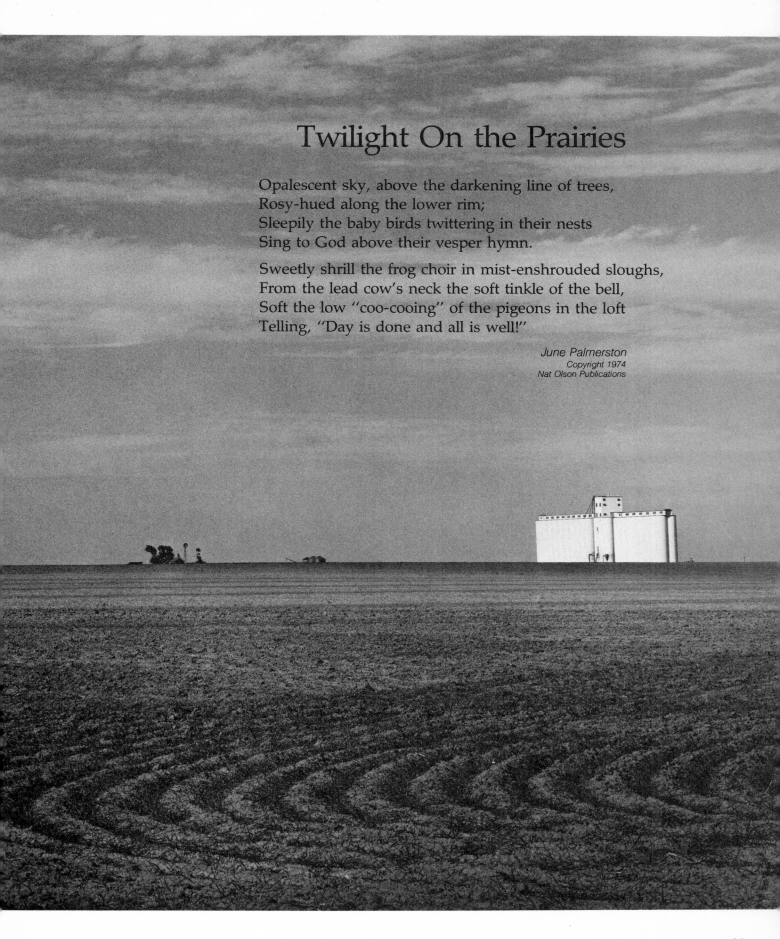

Twilight On the Prairies

Opalescent sky, above the darkening line of trees,
Rosy-hued along the lower rim;
Sleepily the baby birds twittering in their nests
Sing to God above their vesper hymn.

Sweetly shrill the frog choir in mist-enshrouded sloughs,
From the lead cow's neck the soft tinkle of the bell,
Soft the low "coo-cooing" of the pigeons in the loft
Telling, "Day is done and all is well!"

June Palmerston
Copyright 1974
Nat Olson Publications

Water

If percentages mean much, God must value water very highly, for nearly three-quarters of the earth's surface is water — rivers, lakes, oceans. About three-fourths of the weight of the human body is water.

Life could not continue without water. We need it to quench our thirst (nothing satisfies like clear, cold water!).

We need it for cooking (water is an excellent conductor of heat).

We need it for washing (more things dissolve in water than in any other solvent).

We need it for plant life (without irrigation, a desert is a desolate place).

We need it to produce steam to generate power. (Remember Isaac Watts' steam engine of 1795 and Robert Fulton's steamboat of 1807?)

Composed of hydrogen (which burns readily) and oxygen (the gas that causes all other things to burn when ignited), H_2O, water, is constantly used to put out fires. Only God could produce such a miracle! He so firmly combined these two gases that neither one acts independently; instead they act as a coolant, putting the fire below kindling temperature and blocking off the oxygen in the surrounding air.

God Himself refers often to water to illustrate great spiritual truths. In Isaiah 55, verses 10 and 11, the Lord says, "For as the rain cometh down, and the snow from heaven, and returneth not thither, but watereth the earth, and maketh it bring forth and bud, that it may give seed to the sower, and bread to the eater: So shall my word be that goeth forth out of my mouth: it shall not return unto me void, but it shall accomplish that which I please, and it shall prosper *in the thing* whereto I sent it."

Speaking to a spiritually thirsty woman, Jesus said, "But whosoever drinketh of the water that I shall give him shall never thirst; but the water that I shall give him shall be in him a well of water springing up into everlasting life." (John 4:14)

How wonderful that God should give water for both body and spirit!

The wisdom of God is clearly seen in the wonderful way he prepares his creations for what lies before them. His are no last-minute preparations. God prepares a couple for parenthood nine months before the baby's birth. Even prayer is begun in the heart of God before the words come from our mouths. Jesus said, "Your Father knoweth what things ye have need of, before ye ask him." (Matthew 6:8)

When we study the coconut palm, we sense that no human parent could better prepare her children for what lies ahead than does this amazing tree — a native of the coasts and islands of the South Seas.

Opening the coconut we discover a seed carefully surrounded by a shell and husk — the latter made of the hardest wood known. The shell itself is sealed in a waterproof and airtight husk measuring at least two inches thick, made of springy fibrous material.

The reason for all this protection becomes apparent when we see the coconut palm growing its seed in the highest branches — up to 100 feet in the air! When the seed tumbles to the ground from such a height, the fibrous husk, filled with air spaces, acts as an air cushion. Then, when the seed reaches the ocean, it floats as easily as an air-filled rubber raft. No water gets in it because the heavy coating of varnish on the husk makes it completely waterproof. When the seed reaches its destination, often hundreds of miles from its place of origin, the waves toss it up on the beach and the shifting sands bury it.

Before germination can take place, the seed must get moisture. Salt water cannot meet the need of this land tree. The wise parent knew this and did something about it before the seed left home. Inside its shell, she prepacked fresh sweet water which man calls "coconut milk" — enough to last the infant tree for six months.

The Coconut Palm

Apart from God, how does one explain a tree, without any known capacity for thought, preparing its offspring for the big fall to earth, the long ride on the ocean, and survival through its own built-in water supply?

"*Such* knowledge *is* too wonderful for me; it is high, I cannot *attain* unto it," exclaimed the Psalmist.
(Psalm 139:6)

"A tree is known by *his* fruit."
Matthew 12:33

46

The Apple Tree

The apple is "God's Supersalesman" because it appeals to all of the five senses: seeing, hearing, tasting, smelling and touching. The apple looks beautiful, sounds crunchy when bitten into, tastes delicious, smells fragrant and is smooth and easy to hold.

Before we can have good apples, however, there must be good apple trees — *planted* in areas where temperatures register adequate heat and cold (such as Washington State and British Columbia), and *pruned* each year rather than severely cut at irregular intervals.

Jesus referred to the necessity of pruning a fruit tree when He said: "Every branch in me that beareth not fruit he taketh away: and every *branch* that beareth fruit, he purgeth it, that it may bring forth more fruit." (John 15:2)

"A tree is known by *his* fruit." (Matthew 12:33)

The Butterfly

A young boy defined a caterpillar as an "upholstered worm." Well, words do fail anyone to fully explain the excitement and wonder of how a groveling little worm of earth becomes a bright, beautiful butterfly, fluttering in the air.

Let's take a look at the Cecropia moth and see how she changes into one of the loveliest of the silk-spinning variety.

First of all, as a caterpillar she literally gorges herself, week after week, on leafy food until her silk glands are full. Then she makes a thread, five hundred or more yards in length, and winds it around herself in a hammock-shaped cocoon. She attaches it lengthwise to the under side of a twig.

Actually, she weaves a double cocoon, one inside the other. The walls of both are well made and tough, but the inner lining is smooth, so it will not irritate the tender skin of the resident.

The most outstanding feature of the cocoon, however, is a valve-like device where the moth-to-be can make a ready exit. Made at the end of the cocoon, the threads run in the same direction, meet at a point, and double back on themselves, thereby not crossing and sealing the opening. (In the rest of the cocoon, the threads cross and recross, making an exceedingly tough defense against enemies.) Who but God could give a lowly caterpillar such intelligence of engineering design — a valve that opens easily outward from within but not inward from without?

Then there's another wonder to consider: the only business of the Cecropia *caterpillar* is to cut up and chew its food; therefore, God gives it powerful cutting tools in its head. The *moth* does not need such equipment so the Lord gives it a hose-like mouth to suck up sap or nectar from the flowers. If the moth woke up in a cocoon without a door, she would soon die because she would be unable to chew her way out. That's why God caused the caterpillar to make a door *before* she went to sleep!

Finally, in the fullness of time, the moth does come out and wings its way into the breezes — colorful and capable of living the new life!

The Bible speaks of man being transformed — not just physically, like the Cecropia moth, but spiritually through an experience called "the new birth." "If any man *be* in Christ, *he is* a new creature: old things are passed away; behold, all things are become new." (II Corinthians 5:17)

More wonderful than a caterpillar-to-butterfly experience is a sinner-to-saint conversion through the transforming power of Almighty God!

The Honeybee

"O how I love thy law."
Psalm 119:97

"O how I love thy law! it is my meditation all the day . . . How sweet are thy words unto my taste! yea, sweeter than honey to my mouth." So exclaimed the writer of Psalm 119: verses 97 and 103.

What an apt comparison! Honey, the only food produced by an insect suitable for human consumption, is pure, sweet and beneficial to human health. It is to the body what God's law is to the spirit of man.

Let's take a closer look at the insect behind this amazing food — the honeybee.

Is there any of God's creation busier than a bee? For the first two days of adulthood, she cleans the hive. On the third day, she receives a promotion — she feeds the older larvae. On the fifth day, she receives another assignment — to feed the younger larvae. Around the tenth day, her seniority entitles her to receive the food brought in by the field-workers and to place it in cells for storage. On the seventeenth day, her main work becomes that of guarding the hive, with short exploratory flights for a bit of diversion. Finally, on her twenty-first day of life, she becomes a full-fledged field bee, busily gathering food for the hive. Sometimes this involves up to 300 stops to get enough nectar to fill her honey sac.

Honey-making, however, is no solo effort. It is a cooperative matter. After the bee has used its tongue as a straw to sip up the nectar from the heart of a flower, she adds chemicals known as "enzymes" from her own body, then makes a "beeline" (the shortest way possible) for home. There she is greeted by some of the resident workers who, using a mouth-to-mouth method of transfer, move her nectar to the hive workers. They, in turn, store the nectar in the honey cells where more enzymes are added. Certain hive workers then beat their wings furiously, circulating the air so the nectar's excess water will evaporate. As the evaporation continues, the enzymes take effect, producing honey — a unique food needing no refrigeration.

Equally interesting is the bee's manufacturing plant — the hive. Made of beeswax, it contains thousands of cells, all six-sided, enabling the largest number of cells of a given size to fit into a given area without wasting space in the corners.

In each colony, there may be 30,000 to 60,000 bees — a fertile female called "the queen;" some males, "the drones," stingless and non-workers; many infertile females called "workers." Together they make "a beehive of activity."

One more fascinating fact about the beehive. Some years ago, three respected mathematicians — one in Germany, one in Scotland, and the other in France — working independently of each other, used calculus to determine the measurements of two angles in the pyramidal base of a honeybee's cell. Identical results were obtained: 109° 26 min. for the obtuse and 70° 34 min. for the acute. Who but an omnipresent God could cause honeybees all over the world to use the exact specifications for these cells?

The Poppy

Long before medical science alerted the public to the harm tension and strain can cause to the human mind and body, the Psalmist David wrote this recipe for relaxed living, "Commit thy way unto the Lord; trust also in him; and he shall bring it to pass." (Psalm 37:5)

"Commit" and "trust" are the two commands God gives. Then He promises to "bring to pass" whatever we have committed to Him and for which we are daily trusting Him.

When we study the common field poppy, we see that it literally "commits" its seed to the wind God sends, "trusting" that poppies will grow as a result of this commitment. Do poppies "come to pass?" Yes, in abundance. Even "in Flander's Fields the poppies grow."

How does all of this take place?

The secret lies in the unique design of the poppy's receptacle — a globular bowl, complete with lid, divided vertically into many compartments which face every direction.

Because the compartments are closed to each other by distinct partitions, the wind reaches only those on the leeward side of the bowl. The wind lifts the ripe seeds and carries them to their destinations. (Poppy seeds need no sails nor wings like other seeds; they are so light they simply blow with the breeze.)

It is only after the wind has changed direction several times that all the poppy's seeds are on their way to grow and bloom. (If they had all left at the same time, there would have been an "overpoppyulation" in one area and no poppies in other places.)

Another point of interest is the fact that poppy seeds make their exit from the top of the flower. If they left from the part of the bowl closest to the ground, they might drop to the earth in a heap, sprout, then quickly die from malnutrition. God doesn't allow these seeds (32,000 in one variety) to come to such a tragic end. Neither will He fail the person who "commits," "trusts," and waits for Him to bring things "to pass."

"Commit thy way unto the Lord;
trust also in him;
and he shall bring it to pass."

Psalm 37:5

54

The Rose

"The desert shall rejoice, and blossom as the rose."

Isaiah 35:1

"The desert shall rejoice, and blossom as the rose" is the word-picture the Prophet Isaiah painted of Israel's future prosperity. (Isaiah 35:1) What greater contrast is there — a barren desert and a beautiful rose?

Known as the "Queen of Flowers," the rose was the first flower to be cultivated. (It is a descendant of the wild rose — the state flower of New York, North Dakota and Iowa.)

There are 2,000 species in the rose family. The oil used to scent perfumes and cosmetics is called "attar of roses." Over 4,000 roses give their petals to produce one pound of this oil. There is a delightful story told of an imagined conversation between a pathway and a rose.

"Why are you smelling so fragrant today?" the pathway asked.

The rose replied, "A man carelessly stepped on me. I never smell sweeter than when I'm stepped on."

"Not me," snarled the pathway. "The more I'm stepped on, the harder I become."

The Wise Man Solomon likened the promised Messiah to "The Rose of Sharon." (Song of Solomon 2:1) What a fitting description of Jesus Christ, "The Altogether Lovely One!"

Years ago, a devoted follower of Christ, Dr. Howard A. Kelly, the renowned surgeon, wore a lovely rose on the lapel of his coat. When friends would ask the good doctor how his rose could keep fresh for so long, he would smile and show the small glass vial filled with water pinned to the back of his lapel.

"Like the rose," he explained, "a Christian draws refreshment from the Water of Life, Jesus Christ, for beautiful, fragrant Christian living."

"Though your sins be as scarlet, they shall be as white as snow."

Isaiah 1:18

"Hast thou entered into the treasures of the snow?"

Job 38:22

"He giveth snow like wool."

Psalm 147:16

"The snow had begun in the gloaming
And busily all the night
Had been heaping fields and highways
With silence deep and white.

Every pine and fir and hemlock
Wore ermine too dear for an earl,
And the poorest twig in the elm tree
Was ridged inch-deep with pearl."

James Russell Lowell

Snow

"Hast thou entered into the treasures of the snow . . .?" (Job 38:22) "He gives snow like wool." (Psalm 147:16) "Though your sins be as scarlet, they shall be as white as snow." (Isaiah 1:18)

Purity, protection and an infinite "storehouse" of artistic designs — this is how the Bible describes the white, fluffy substance which transforms barren branches and bleak fields into "a winter wonderland." In a similarly miraculous way, God transforms barren lives into something beautiful, gives his protection, and makes the recipient amazed at the wonders of his love.

A snowflake is an amazing work of art. It is six-pointed, each perfectly set at a 60-degree angle. Although every snowflake is hexagonal (six-pointed), each bears a different design. Who but God could create 1,000 billion flakes (the estimated amount that fall in an average snowstorm) to be so alike and yet so different?

The way a snowflake is formed is equally fascinating. Particles of water vapor in a cloud unite to form six-pointed crystals. These, in turn, find something to which they can cling — the dust of the air, salt particles, bacteria, or even star dust! As these particles of water vapor condense around the dust nuclei, the six-pointed ice crystals form and go tumbling about rubbing and striking each other. Each minute splinter of ice becomes a nucleus, attracting more water molecules and producing, in turn, a new snowflake.

As the new snowflake drifts downward, it forms fernlike arms from each corner. Then branching crystals grow from the arms until they touch and join. Finally the flake becomes so heavy that it leaves the cloud and falls to earth.

When billions of such flakes descend, the barren field becomes a dazzling snowscape! In addition, the layer of snow becomes a thermal insulator, conserving the heat of the earth and protecting vegetables from the severe winter cold.

God, the "Master Designer," knows just how to combine beauty and practicality, doesn't He?

Cotton

Man is happy if he can invent a tool or a machine which has *two* uses instead of one. When God made the cotton plant, though, he blessed it with *many* uses. Foremost, of course, is its fibre. Its oil is used as a base for margarine, shortening, salad oil, soap and other products. Any seeds left over make good cattle feed. There may be many more uses forthcoming when chemists announce new discoveries from this versatile plant.

Cotton has been valued and used for thousands of years. Way back in the time of Queen Esther, we read that "there were white cotton curtains" in the palace of King Ahasuerus.

American history recounts the long, hard days of pickers who went from one plantation to another during the harvest days of August to November, carrying large gunny sacks over their shoulders. They used both hands to pick the cotton bolls. When the sacks were filled, they were weighed, then emptied into a wagon. Each picker was paid according to the number of pounds of cotton he had picked. Approximately 70 bolls of cotton make one pound.

In 1793, Eli Whitney's cotton gin revolutionized the cotton industry — clearing as much cotton from seeds as 50 men could do by hand.

The next time we put on a cotton shirt or skirt, or use margarine or salad oil with cotton oil as the base, let us praise our Creator, knowing afresh that "Every good gift and every perfect gift is from above, and cometh down from the Father of lights." (James 1:17)

Cotton is one of the "good gifts" God has given man!

Grapes

Delicious to eat, or to drink of its juice, delightful to look at and hold, the grape is one of the most popular creations from God's hand.

"I am the vine, ye *are* the branches."

John 15:5

When Leif Ericson, in 1000 A.D., was driven off course on his way to Greenland to share the Christian faith with the colony established by his father, Eric the Red, he landed in an area where wild grapes grew in abundance. Leif named this part of the world, "Vinland," which historians believe is a part of what is now known as the coast of New England. The wild grapes he found were the forerunners of today's beautiful Concord grapes.

Although the Concord variety thrives on the east coast of the United States of America, it does poorly on the west coast where the grapes from the Old World thrive in the mild winters and dry growing season. California is the most productive state for grape growing in the United States. The world's greatest vineyards, however, are not found in America, but in the countries huddled around the Mediterranean Sea.

Because the grape figures so prominently in the history of this part of the world, it is not surprising to discover the Bible speaking so often of this fruit. When the Israeli spies came back from searching the land of Canaan, they brought "a branch with one cluster of grapes" that was so heavy that "they bare it between two upon a staff." (Numbers 13:23) In New Testament times, Jesus established "The Lord's Supper" (better known as "The Communion"). He chose "the fruit of the vine" as one of the two sacraments with which to remember His sacrifice on Calvary.

Before He left the disciples to return to His Father, Jesus reminded them of their continued dependence upon Him. "I am the vine, ye *are* the branches. He that abideth in me, and I in him, the same bringeth forth much fruit; for without me, ye can do nothing." (John 15:5)

Mountains

"As the mountains *are* round about Jerusalem, so the Lord *is* round about his people from henceforth even for ever."

Psalm 125:2

With those words, the Psalmist describes the security a child of God feels. Mountains are lofty and inspiring; so is God! Mountains are unmovable, always there. So is God!

Mountains are prominent in the Bible, in both the Old and New Testaments. Moses conversed with God on Mount Sinai and came down with the Ten Commandments. Jesus Christ, pressed by the restless crowds, went up into a mountain to teach his disciples the famed Beatitudes. A mountain symbolizes a place of retreat, where the spirit of man can commune uninterrupted with its Creator.

Psalm 11:1 says, "In the Lord put I my trust: how say ye to my soul, Flee *as* a bird to your mountain?"

In modern times, mountaineering has gained world-wide popularity. Mountain climbers feel well repaid as they view the panorama from a peak thousands of feet high. (In Canada alone, there are more than 100 peaks over 10,000 feet in altitude!) India's Mount Everest, the highest peak, is 29,028 feet. Mount Blanc, climbed in 1786, is 15,782 feet — the highest of the Alps. The Matterhorn, 14,780 feet, was conquered in 1865.

In North America, the highest peak is Mount McKinley, towering 20,300 feet above the Alaskan terrain. Second highest is Mount Logan in the Yukon Territory — 19,850 feet!

With such mammoth visual aids, we must exclaim with the Psalmist, "I will lift up mine eyes unto the hills, from whence cometh my help. My help *cometh* from the Lord, which made heaven and earth." (Psalm 121:1 and 2)

64

The Christmas Tree

The most common Christmas tree is the pine. It grows in abundance in more places than any other type of tree. Often, the pine grows where no other tree will even take root.

Consider the white pine, for example. It grows straight and tall because it sends out two kinds of roots: one for nourishment, the other to act as props to hold the tree upright with the trunk directly over the center of gravity.

The Psalmist David compared "the blessed man" to being "like a tree planted by the rivers of water, that bringeth forth his fruit in his season; his leaf also shall not wither; and whatsoever he doeth shall prosper." (Psalm 1:3)

A German Christmas carol exclaims:

> "O Christmas tree, O Christmas tree,
> Thy leaves are so unchanging.
> Not only green when summer's here,
> But also when 'tis cold and clear.
> O Christmas tree! O Christmas tree!
> Thy leaves are so unchanging!"

How wonderful that God designed a tree that is green even in the winter months when we celebrate Christ's coming to earth! Wouldn't it be difficult to imagine a Christmas gathering without a tree decked with shimmering icicles and multicolored lights?

"A merry heart doeth good *like* a medicine," wrote Solomon, the wisest man who ever lived. (Proverbs 17:22) Wise men through the centuries have heartily agreed.

Abraham Lincoln said, "With the fearful strain that is on me night and day, if I did not laugh I should die."

"I am persuaded that every time a man smiles, but much more when he laughs, it adds something to this fragment of life."
— Sterne

The following are some choice selections of wit and humor — to relax the facial muscles and stir the gift of laughter within the heart.

Definition of Anatomy (by a young boy)

"Your head is kind of round and hard, and your brains are in it. Your hair is on it. Your face is the front of your head where you eat and make faces. Your neck is what keeps your head out of your collar. It is hard to keep clean. Your stomach is something that if you don't eat enough it hurts, and spinach don't help none. Your spine is a long bone in your back that keeps you from folding up. Your back is always behind you no matter how quickly you turn around. Your arms you have to pitch with and so you can reach the butter. Your fingers stick out of your hand so you can throw a curve and add up 'rithmetic. Your legs are what if you have not got two of you can't get to first base. Your feet are what you run on; your toes are what always get stubbed. And that's all there is to you except what's inside and I never saw it."

* Speaking of cooperation, even freckles would make a great suntan *if* they could only get together!

* An atheist is a man with no visible means of support.

* It wasn't the apple in the tree that caused the trouble. It was the pair on the ground!

The Gift of Laughter

* "Mom," asked five-year-old Freddie, "why didn't God put the vitamins in ice cream instead of in spinach?"

* The codfish lays ten thousand eggs; the humble hen lays one . . .
    But the codfish never cackles to tell you what she's done . . .
    And so we scorn the codfish while the humble hen we prize . . .
    Which simply goes to show you that it pays to advertise!

* Asked why his aged grandmother read the Bible so much, Johnny answered, "Oh, I think she's cramming for her finals!"

* A teen-ager protested to his father that ants are not as hard working as people think they are. "Why, they always have time to go to picnics!" he concluded.

* The twenty-year-old photographer took a picture of Grandpa Jones on his 99th birthday. As he left, he said, "Well, Grandpa, I hope I'll be able to take your picture when you're 100."

"I see no reason why you shouldn't be able to," drawled Grandpa. "You look healthy enough!"

* "God has a sense of humor. That's why He made the monkey and some of you fellows!"
— *Billy Sunday*

"A good laugh is sunshine in a house."

Thackeray

Parental Love

Without parental love and discipline, man becomes a rebel, incapable of fully appreciating the beauties of God's creation. We owe a great debt, therefore, to godly parents who taught us, by word and by example, that "beauty is in the eye of the beholder," parents who emphasized honesty, respect for others, and self-control so that our minds and eyes would be clear to see and comprehend God in creation.

The Wise Man, Solomon, wrote, "My son, hear the instruction of thy father, and forsake not the law of thy mother." (Proverbs 1:8) Another wise man remembered his father as a "Mount Sinai" of law and his mother as a "Mount Calvary" of love. He felt that law and love are the two basic guidelines for successful living.

To parents who skillfully combine these two qualities, our hearts say: "Thank you, Mom, thank you, Dad, for showing us the way to enjoy the abundant life which Christ came to bring."

Are All the Children In?

I think ofttimes as the night draws nigh
Of an old house on the hill,
Of a yard all wide and blossom-starred
Where the children played at will.
And when the night at last came down,
Hushing the merry din,
Mother would look around and ask,
"Are all the children in?"

'Tis many and many a year since then,
And the old house on the hill
No longer echoes to childish feet,
And the yard is still, so still.
But I see it all, as the shadows creep,
And though many the years have been
Since then, I can hear Mother ask,
"Are all the children in?"

I wonder if when the shadows fall
On the last short, earthly day,
When we say goodbye to the world outside,
All tired with our childish play,
When we step out into that Other Land
Where Mother so long has been,
Will we hear her ask, just as of old,
"Are all the children in?"

Author Unknown

National Parks

The National Park system of the United States of America includes nearly 300 preserved areas, such as monuments, historic sites, seashores, lakeshores and parks.

Yellowstone National Park was the first to be established. Since then, 1872, scores of other parks have been added until today they total 47,000 square miles — larger than the state of Pennsylvania.

Each park has a beauty and uniqueness of its own. Yellowstone features hot geysers, the most famous of which is Old Faithful, erupting about every 65 minutes. There are also thundering waterfalls plunging into deep gorges and sparkling lakes among the snow-capped mountains. The Grand Canyon is breathtaking in its grandeur, with mile-deep walls of black, brown, lavender and red. Yosemite is the home of spectacular waterfalls, including Yosemite Falls, one of the world's highest. Across the border, in Alberta, Canada, Banff National Park attracts three-quarters of a million tourists annually to its stunning alpine scenery — 2,564 square miles of lofty rocky mountains. There are also two hot sulphur springs for bathing and health purposes.

These parks, and many, many others are reminders of the Edenic bliss earth once knew — beauty, purity, and uninterrupted peace.
As you try to absorb the handiwork of God in the following pages, you will better understand why at creation, "God saw every thing that he had made, and, behold, *it was* very good." (Genesis 1:31)

"I will lift up mine eyes unto the hills, from whence cometh my help. My help *cometh* from the Lord, which made heaven and earth."

Psalm 121:1 and 2

Yosemite

Yellowstone

"**The Lord's compassions fail not.** *They are* **new every morning: great** *is* **thy faithfulness!"**

Lamentations 3:22 and 23

Banff

"O Lord, how manifold are thy works!
in wisdom hast thou made them all:
the earth is full of thy riches."

Psalm 104:24

Grand Canyon

Man

"For what shall it profit a man, if he shall gain the whole world, and lose his own soul?"

Mark 8:36

On the sixth day of creation, God made man — the crown of all his handiwork! He did not simply speak man into being by commanding, "Let there be!" Rather, he said, "Let us make man in our image, after our likeness: and let them have dominion over . . . all the earth." (Genesis 1:26)

The Psalmist David marveled at God's creation of man. "Thy hands have made me and fashioned me." (Psalm 119:73) "Thou hast made man little lower than the angels, and hast crowned him with glory and honor. Thou madest him to have dominion over the works of thy hands; thou hast put all *things* under his feet." (Psalm 8:5 and 6)

By an act of willful disobedience, man lost this original dominion. He does, however, still bear the stamp of having been made in the very image of God. Man is self-conscious; he feels his individuality as a person. He becomes *educated,* not merely trained. He progresses through *choices,* not instincts. He appreciates creative things such as art and music. He has the power of intelligent speech and can express the emotions of sadness and joy, guilt and forgiveness. He is an immortal soul with a thirst for fulfillment that can never be quenched by his few short years on planet earth.

Jesus asked, "For what shall it profit a man, if he shall gain the whole world, and lose his own soul?" (Mark 8:36)

"Oh that *men* would praise the Lord *for* his goodness, and *for* his wonderful works to the children of men!"

Psalm 107:8

A Man and a Woman

Because man was created a social being, his heart desired someone with whom to share his life. God responded by making woman. The Living Bible vividly describes the event in these words: "And the Lord God said, 'It isn't good for man to be alone; I will make a companion for him, a helper suited to his needs.' So the Lord God formed from the soil every kind of animal and bird, and brought them to the man to see what he would call them; and whatever he called them, that was their name. But still there was no proper helper for the man. Then the Lord God caused the man to fall into a deep sleep, and took one of his ribs and closed up the place from which he had removed it, and made the rib into a woman, and brought her to the man. 'This is it!' Adam exclaimed. 'She is part of my own bone and flesh! Her name is 'woman' because she was taken out of a man.' This explains why a man leaves his father and mother and is joined to his wife in such a way that the two become one person." (Genesis 2:18 and 24)*

Comments Matthew Henry, "Woman was taken out of man; not out of his head to top him, nor out of his feet to be trampled underfoot, but out of his side to be equal with him, under his arm to be protected and near to his heart to be beloved."

* From the Living Bible, permission of Tyndale House Publishers.

As wonderful as marital love is, however, it can never completely fill the God-shaped vacuum in the human heart. . .

Jesus Christ

JESUS BEFORE PILATE

That is why
"God so loved the world, that he gave
his only begotten Son, that whosoever believeth in
him should not perish, but have everlasting life."
(John 3:16)

Charles Spurgeon often said, "If you cannot travel,
remember that our Lord Jesus Christ is more glorious than
all else you could ever see. Get a view of Christ and you
have seen more than mountains and cascades and valleys
and seas can ever show you. Earth can give its beauty,
and stars their brightness, but all these put together can
never rival Him."

Jesus Christ, "the Altogether Lovely One,"
gives this beautiful invitation: "Come unto
me, all *ye* that labor and are heavy laden, and
I will give you rest." (Matthew 11:28)

Praise Ye the Lord!

Praise ye the Lord. Praise God in his sanctuary: praise him in the firmament of his power.

Praise him for his mighty acts: praise him according to his excellent greatness.

Praise him with the sound of the trumpet: praise him with the psaltery and harp.

Praise him with the timbrel and dance: praise him with stringed instruments and organs.

Praise him upon the loud cymbals: praise him upon the high sounding cymbals.

Let everything that hath breath praise the Lord. Praise ye the Lord.

Psalm 150

HOW GREAT THOU ART!

Index